*Leader's Guide
for grou*

Compassionate

Warren W. Wiersbe

Leader's Guide prepared by
LAMOYNE SCHNEIDER

Eight Multiuse Transparency Masters (for visual aids) are included in a removable center section. Instructions for using the Multiuse Transparency Masters are on pages 4–5.

VICTOR BOOKS
A DIVISION OF SCRIPTURE PRESS PUBLICATIONS INC.
USA CANADA ENGLAND

ISBN: 0-89693-592-2
© 1988 by SP Publications, Inc. All rights reserved
Printed in the United States of America

VICTOR BOOKS
A division of SP Publications, Inc.
      Wheaton, Illinois 60187

General Preparation

Before you tear into this leader's guide in all the excitement of preparing for session 1, take time to read pages 3-6.

If you are a little unsure of yourself because you're leading a group of adults for the first time, then follow the simple steps of FOCUS, DISCOVER, RESPOND outlined for each session.

FOCUS will arouse interest and focus your group's attention on the session topic. DISCOVER dynamically involves your group so that they can discover God's truth and its implications for their lives. RESPOND helps group members apply God's truth to their lives.

Even if you're a "veteran" adult group leader who has led multitudes in studies such as this before, this leader's guide can also help you. Simply skim the text for each session and choose the basic lesson parts that will aid you in your personal strategy.

Back to Basics

Read the entire text and this leader's guide. Underline important passages in the text and make notes as ideas come to you. Note any activities in the guide that take advance planning or preparation.

As leader, your enthusiasm for the subject and your personal interest in those you lead, will in large measure determine the interest and response of your group.

Plan to use teaching aids such as a chalkboard or an overhead projector during each session. If neither of these tools is available, use a magic marker on large sheets of newsprint.

Encourage group members to bring their Bibles to each session and use them. It is good to have several modern-speech translations on hand for purposes of comparison.

Getting Started Right

Start on time. This is especially important for the first session because it will set the pattern for the rest of the course.

Begin with prayer, asking the Holy Spirit to open hearts and minds and to give understanding so that the truth will be applied.

Involve everyone. Group involvement is a key to learning. As learners, we retain only 10% of what we hear, 20% of what we see, 65% of what we hear and see, BUT 90% of what we hear, see, and do.

Promote a relaxed environment. Arrange your chairs in a circle or semicircle. This promotes eye contact among members and encourages more dynamic discussion. Be relaxed in your own attitude and manner. As leader, address people by name to help others get acquainted.

Adapting the Course

This material is designed for quarterly use on a weekly basis, but it may be readily adapted to different uses. To use the course over a 12- to 13-week period, simply follow the lesson arrangement as it is given in this guide. Combine sessions if you have fewer weeks in which to cover the material. In some ways, this guide is like a smorgasbord of teaching ideas. As leader, *you* must pick and choose those activities in each session that will best satisfy the spiritual needs of your group members. You can't possibly expect them to digest it all!

A Final Word

Be motivated to master your subject so that you can be the kind of teacher Solomon describes in Ecclesiastes 12:10: *For the Preacher was not only a wise man, but a good teacher; he not only taught what he knew to the people, but taught them in an interesting manner (The Living Bible,* © 1971, Tyndale House Publishers).

MTM Instructions

"What's an MTM?" you ask. It's a Multiuse Transparency Master. Several MTMs are provided for you in the removable center section of this guide; MTMs are designed to increase your teaching impact.

The Victor Multiuse Transparency Masters in this guide will help you enliven your sessions and transmit vital information to the mind through the eye-gate, tying in with educators' recognition of the teaching value of visual aids. They are numbered consecutively (MTM-1—MTM-10) and show with what sessions they should be used. The guide gives specific directions for when and how to use each MTM in the lesson material.

Mechanics

Remove the center section of this guide by opening up the staples in the center. Lift the illustration sheets out and then close the staples again to keep the remaining portion of the guide together. To protect and flatten the MTMs, store them in a regular file folder.

Making Transparencies

You can make your own overhead transparencies inexpensively through the use of these transparency masters. This can be done in at least three ways:

1. *Thermal copier* (an infrared heat transfer process). This is probably the fastest way to make a transparency. Follow the instructions that come with the

copier equipment. Note that the color portions of the MTM are designed *not* to reproduce.

2. *Electrostatic process* (such as Xerox). Make sure that you use the correct film for the right machine. Some color on the MTM will come out gray. On certain MTMs some information, printed in a special light color, will *not* reproduce on machine-made transparencies. This gives you extra information to share orally or to fill in during the session.

3. *Trace your own MTM.* With minimum artistic ability, you can place a sheet of transparent film over the MTM and trace the major parts of the illustration. Exactness is not necessary. For best results, use clear 8½ x 11 sheets of polyester or mylar film (acetate works, but curls). By tracing your own transparencies, you add to your teaching options by being able to make overlays which can be used in a progressive, visually effective way.

Other Uses of Transparency Masters

1. *Visuals.* For small groups, use the MTMs just as they are, as printed visual aids. Or, if you put the MTMs inside clear "report covers," you can write on them.

2. *Spirit masters or mimeo stencils.* From these masters or stencils you can run off material for each group member. Both of these can be made on a 3M Thermofax copier.

Materials Resources

Check with an art supply store for materials such as fiber-tip transparency pens and polyester or mylar film sheets.

A number of distributors carry hundreds of products that can help to make your teaching more effective and fun—for you and your group. If an art store can't supply your needs, try one of these distributors:

Dick Blick Co., Box 1267, Galesburg, IL 61401 • 309/343-6181; or 215/965-6051 (East Coast); or 702/451-7662 (West Coast).

Faith Venture Visuals, Inc., 510 East Main St., Lititz, PA 17543 • 717/626-8503.

Nasco Arts & Crafts, 901 Janesville Ave., Fort Atkinson, WI 53538 • 414/563-2446; or *Nasco West,* 1524 Princeton Ave., Modesto, CA 95352 • 209/529-6957.

SESSION 1

Hear the Good News

TEXT, CHAPTER 1

A QUICK LOOK

Session Topic   We should respond positively when God promises or acts.

Session Goals   You will help group members:
1. Discuss the various responses people have to good news *(Focus)*.
2. Examine the responses to the foretelling of the births of John the Baptist and Jesus *(Discover)*.
3. Resolve to react with faith and praise when God promises or takes action *(Respond)*.

GETTING READY

What You'll Need
Bible
Be Compassionate
Refreshments
Newspaper *(Focus #2)*
MTM-1
Paper, pencils

Getting Ready to Teach
1. Obtain copies of Warren Wiersbe's *Be Compassionate* for your group members. Before the first session, distribute books and tell members to read chapter 1 of the text and Luke 1.
2. Arrange for simple refreshments, such as coffee or juice and doughnuts.
3. Find a newspaper with a photo of the President of the United States on the front page. With a black marker, print a false headline on a strip of paper—"President to Visit Hometown." Then glue the head-

7

line above the President's picture. (If you can't find a front page with the President's picture on it, cut one from another source and glue it on the front page with the headline.)
4. Complete the reading assignment yourself, noting in Luke and in Wiersbe the responses to the foretelling of the births of John the Baptist and Jesus. Then skim the rest of Wiersbe, reading the chapter titles to get a feel for the book.
5. Make one copy of MTM-1. Cut it into four sections along the dotted lines.
6. Pray for your group members and for the spiritual success of the study. Do all assignments along with the group; be spiritually ready for and on top of each session.

THE LESSON

FOCUS

1. As group members arrive, greet them and direct them to the refreshments. Allow the first 15 minutes of the session for members to get acquainted. Have everyone take a seat. For introductions ask members to give their names and tell the best news they have heard in the past week. You go first.

2. When all have shared, say: **I have some good news of a kind to tell you about.** Hold up the newspaper so the picture and headline are visible. Say: **Even though the President's visit is some weeks away, people in his hometown are already responding to the news. What do you suppose the response would be of local school children whose teachers have talked about the importance of the President?** (General excitement, hopes for autographs or pictures) **What about the mayor of the city?** (Feeling of importance as he will officially welcome the President) **Citizens who voted for him?** (Warm acceptance, support) **Citizens who voted for his opponents?** (Curiosity, apathy, aloofness) **The hometown police?** (Nervousness, irritation at being subject to federal security personnel during the visit) Point out to group members that the same news can bring a variety of responses.

DISCOVER

1. Divide the group into four discovery groups. Give each group one of the four sections of MTM-1, a piece of paper, and a pencil. Say: **Your**

discovery group will read the passage on the slip I gave you, discuss the questions, take notes, and share your findings with us all. You may refer to chapter 1 of *Be Compassionate* if you wish. Allow 10 minutes for this exercise. Then call for brief reports.

2. If the point comes up, ask: **Why was Zacharias' question "How can I be sure of this?" different from Mary's "How will this be?"**

===== RESPOND =====

1. As the discussion ends, pull these points together:

☐ Zacharias' initial response of unbelief resulted when he considered his (and his wife's) physical age instead of the power of God.

☐ Mary responded in faith to Gabriel's announcement because of her humility and because she recognized that she was simply the handmaid or bondslave of the Lord.

☐ Elizabeth, John, and Mary responded to the coming of Jesus with joy. Mary magnified God in her song for what He did for her, for all His people, and for Israel.

☐ At John's birth, Zacharias responded with praise to God for redeeming His people as He promised.

2. Explain to group members that good news calls for a positive response. Ask members to think back to the good news they shared with the group during introductions. Ask: **When you heard this good news, what was your response? Did you even have a response? Now when you hear of God acting or promising to act, what is your response? Faith? Unbelief? Joy? Indifference? Praise?** Pause slightly between these questions so members can evaluate.

3. Challenge them to respond to the Lord with faith, joy, and praise. Close by praying that the Holy Spirit will help them do so this coming week.

===== ASSIGNMENT =====

1. Have group members read chapter 2 of the text and Luke 2 for next week.

2. Ask four group members to participate in a role play for the next session.

SESSION 2

The Lord Is Come

TEXT, CHAPTER 2

A QUICK LOOK

Session Topic Joseph and Mary and Jesus modeled obedience to God's Law and civil authority.

Session Goals You will help group members:
1. Be made aware that there are laws they should obey *(Focus)*.
2. Identify ways that Joseph and Mary and Jesus obeyed God's laws and man's law *(Discover)*.
3. Decide to follow their example of obedience *(Respond)*.

GETTING READY

What You'll Need
Bible
Be Compassionate
Paper, pencils

Getting Ready to Teach
1. Read chapter 2 of the text and Luke 2. Though the Scripture contains very familiar episodes, read them as if for the first time.
2. Before the session begins, meet with the group members who agreed to participate in the role plays. Assign the following four parts: Mr. Bisbee, a game warden, Mrs. Bisbee, a traffic officer. Then read through the role plays, allowing your players to rehearse their parts. If possible, provide your players with a few simple props—a badge, official-looking cap, fishing pole, and so on.
3. Note especially where Joseph and Mary, and Jesus as well, submitted themselves to the law and au-

thority over them.
4. Bring a couple sheets of paper to put out as the session ends so members can write their names and phone numbers as they leave.
5. When you are directed to lead a discussion, encourage members not only to express their own opinions but to react to those of other members. They may agree, disagree, or add to what others have said. Since the discussion questions come from you, it is natural that members direct answers back to you. But try to get members talking with each other, not just with you.

THE LESSON

=== FOCUS ===

1. As the group assembles, find out the names of newcomers so you can introduce them to the others. Do so as the session opens.

2. Ask if anyone can introduce those from the first session for the sake of the newcomers (or for the sake of everyone, for that matter). The point is to let members hear names that they can attach to the faces in the group.

3. Ask your role players to come forward and perform the following role plays.

In the first role play, a game warden (indicate player) meets Mr. Bisbee (indicate player) while Bisbee is fishing, and asks to see his fishing license. Bisbee, who cannot produce a license, produces excuses instead.

Let the role play continue for a few minutes. Thank the game warden for participating; that person sits down while Bisbee stays in the front of the group.

Ask Mrs. Bisbee to join Mr. Bisbee for the second role play.

In the second role play, Mr. Bisbee intends to buy a $5 child's circus ticket for his 13-year-old daughter instead of an $8 adult ticket, even though children's tickets are for those 12 years or under. His wife confronts him in the ticket line and he justifies his action.

Thank Mrs. Bisbee afterward and have her be seated. Ask the traffic officer to come forward.

For the third role play, a traffic officer has just pulled Bisbee over for driving 45 mph in a 30 mph zone. In the course of trying to weasel out of a ticket, it comes out that Bisbee was hurrying to the deacon's meeting at church. Bisbee is "seated in his car" while the officer stands nearby.

Thank your traffic officer and Mr. Bisbee especially for taking part in the role plays.

11

DISCOVER

1. Distribute paper and pencils to the group. Say: **Common people, like Mr. Bisbee—like all of us, in fact—are subject to the law and to authority. But suppose you were very important or powerful. Surely then you could do virtually whatever you wanted to. What if you were parents of the Messiah, or the Messiah Himself. If anyone deserved exemption from the law and authority, it would be them, right?**

As these passages are read, however, jot down ways that Joseph and Mary, and Jesus as well, submitted themselves obediently to God's Law and civil authorities. You can follow in your Bibles in Luke 2, if you wish. Ask for three persons to read these passages aloud: Luke 2:1-5, 21-32, and 39-52.

2. Have the readers read slowly and distinctly. When they finish, call for observations from the others. Make sure the following points are brought up:

☐ Joseph and Mary obeyed the census decree and went to Bethlehem to register;

☐ Joseph and Mary took Jesus to be circumcised eight days after birth;

☐ Joseph and Mary observed the time of purification according to the Law of Moses;

☐ Joseph and Mary presented Jesus as the firstborn son to the Lord in the temple in Jerusalem, and offered a sacrifice according to the Law of the Lord;

☐ Joseph and Mary returned to Nazareth after doing everything required by the Law of the Lord;

☐ Joseph and Mary attended the Passover feast according to the custom of the Law;

☐ Jesus returned to Nazareth with Joseph and Mary and was obedient to them.

3. Initiate a discussion with these questions:

☐ **What are your impressions of this family regarding obedience?**

☐ **Why were Joseph and Mary careful to obey the Law of the Lord and the civil authorities?**

☐ **What makes their obedience different from that of the Pharisees of the day?**

☐ **To what extent should Christians be model citizens?**

4. Read Matthew 5:17-18 and Galatians 4:4. Then ask: **Why did God choose to send the Saviour to us under the law, not above it?**

RESPOND

1. Ask: **What are the implications for us of the example of Joseph and Mary and Jesus? How can we put this emphasis into action this week?**

Take suggestions and encourage practicality.

2. Say: **While born-again Christians are under grace instead of law, they should keep the Ten Commandments out of love for God, in order to give a positive witness in the world, to keep their own spiritual lives healthy, and guard the reputation and purity of the body of Christ, the church. Believers do well to obey the laws of the land too, so far as they don't countermand the Law of God.**

3. Have group members pair up with one other person and share situations where their obedience to God's Law or civil authority should improve. Then ask the pairs to pray for each other for forgiveness and for the determination to obey when they should. Allow as much time as is needed. Close in prayer when everyone is finished.

===== ASSIGNMENT =====

1. Have group members read chapter 3 of the text and Luke 3–4 for next week.

2. Ask members to write their names and phone numbers as they leave on one of the sheets of paper you have put out.

SESSION 3

This Is the Son of God

TEXT, CHAPTER 3

A QUICK LOOK

Session Topic   The divine sonship of Jesus has compelling witnesses.

Session Goals   You will help group members:
1. Acknowledge the impact of authoritative witnesses *(Focus)*.
2. Examine the witnesses to the sonship of Jesus *(Discover)*.
3. Strengthen their own verbal witness with a tangible reminder *(Response)*.

GETTING READY

What
You'll Need

Bible
Be Compassionate
Two vases *(Focus #2)*
Tape player
Copies of MTM-2
Pencils

Getting Ready
to Teach

1. Read chapter 3 of the text and Luke 3-4.
2. Make copies of MTM-2 for group members.
3. In the Focus section, you will need two objects that could be, with some persuasion and imagination, taken for antiques or valuable pieces—for example, two vases (or whatever) that are as similar as possible in appearance. For one of the vases, type a brief, authentic-looking document from the North American Antique Association attesting to the fact that the vase was once owned by George and Martha Washington. Put an "official seal" on the docu-

ment. Tape-record a brief interview with an "expert" in early American antiques where he states that, having examined the vase personally, he is convinced that it is not only authentic, but is the only one of its kind. "Create" a bill of sale showing that the vase sold in auction in New York City last year for $20,000. Finally, cut out a newspaper article which you will pretend to read which describes a break-in at the art gallery where the vase was displayed. The thief went straight for the vase, but was frightened away before he could open its case. You will bring no documents whatsoever for the second vase.

THE LESSON

FOCUS

1. Try to greet group members by name since this will help them feel that they belong.

2. Display the two vases (or whatever) side by side in the front of the room. Say: **These vases may look similar but they are worlds apart in their value. The vase on the left is actually an antique worth a small fortune. But don't take my word for it—this vase has its own papers.** Show and read the letter from the North American Antique Association. Then play the recorded interview with the early American antique expert. Next, show the bill of sale from last year's auction. Last of all, pretend to read the article about the attempted theft of the vase, filling in suitable details. Keep from passing around the papers since it may dilute the effect. Say: **So that is the vase on the left. Frankly, I know nothing about the vase on the right: where it comes from, its age or value—nothing.**

3. Address one member and say: **Suppose you wanted to spend $25,000 on one of these vases as an investment. Which one would you pick? Why did you pick the vase on the left? What convinced you it was the genuine article? What about the rest of you—what influence did the documentation and other evidence have on your choice?**

DISCOVER

1. When members have adequately answered these questions, say: **If we are going to invest heavily in anything, we must be sure the object of our investment is genuine. These articles (the authenticating letter, the witness of the antiques expert, the bill of sale, and even the article on the**

near theft of the vase) would help convince a buyer he was getting a true antique. Point out that God has given us evidence in Scripture—reliable witnesses—to testify that Jesus is in fact His Son. In this way, followers of Jesus would be convinced of His divine sonship.

2. Have the group divide into five discovery groups. Then hand out a copy of MTM-2 to all and a pencil for each group's secretary. Assign a group to each witness. Groups will read their Scriptures and discuss the questions. Chapter 3 of the text may be used and notes can be taken on the MTM.

3. When the discovery groups have finished, each may take 2 minutes to share with the whole group its answers to the questions, plus additional insights about these witnesses to the divine sonship of Jesus.

4. After the last group has shared, ask: **When you consider the witnesses of the Scripture, John the Baptist, the Holy Spirit, God the Father, and even Satan and the demons to the fact that Jesus is the Son of God, how does it affect your faith, and why?**

RESPOND

1. In general, the testimony of these key witnesses should have a confirming, encouraging effect on the faith of group members. Explain to the group that these witnesses have enabled Christians through the centuries to profess Jesus as the Son of God. Say: **Occasionally we hear people express doubt that Jesus is God's son. For times like this, keep these witnesses and references in your Bible so you'll know where to find them.** Suggest that they can tear off the bottom half of the handout and keep it in their Bibles, or write the information on a back page of their Bibles. Say: **With a tangible reminder like this, your witness to doubters or seekers can be stronger.**

2. Close in prayer, thanking God for having recorded in Luke these testimonies that Jesus truly is His Son.

ASSIGNMENT

1. Have group members read chapter 4 of the text and Luke 5 for next week.

2. Ask them to come prepared next week to share about meeting individuals who brought about significant positive change in their lives.

SESSION 4

The Difference Jesus Makes

TEXT, CHAPTER 4

A QUICK LOOK

Session Topic   Encountering Jesus with faith changes a person in positive and profound ways.

Session Goals   You will help group members:
1. Recall encounters with others that changed their lives for the better *(Focus)*.
2. List ways that Jesus changed Peter, the leper, the paralytic, and Matthew *(Discover)*.
3. Ask the Lord to continue changing them in needed ways *(Respond)*.

GETTING READY

What You'll Need
Bible
Be Compassionate
Copies of MTM-3
Chalkboard, chalk

Getting Ready to Teach
1. Read chapter 4 of the text, highlighting the author's main points. Also read Luke 5.
2. Make copies of MTM-3 for group members.
3. Think back over your own experience and recall an encounter with someone that led to positive change in your life. That person might be a teacher, a neighbor, a minister, a stranger, or someone well known in his field. You will be first to share, so give it some thought. Each person's sharing should include the change that occurred, and should be limited to two minutes (yours too) so that more can contribute.

17

THE LESSON

FOCUS

1. Say: **At the close of last week's session, I asked you to think of an encounter you had with someone that led to significant positive change in your life.** That person could be a teacher, a neighbor, a minister, a stranger, or someone well known in his field, for example. We'll share some stories about these persons and the changes that occurred to begin our session. Let's limit our sharing to two minutes so we can hear from more members. I'll go first.
2. When finished, call for volunteers. Let the sharing continue for 12 minutes or so—longer if it is going well. Thank those who speak.
3. Ask group members to think of the encounters they've heard about today. Say: **Let's list the needed elements that the life-changers gave us or brought us, and the general areas in which we changed.**
4. List needed elements on the left half of the chalkboard and the areas of change on the right as the members give them. Needed elements may include love or caring; healing or encouragement; direction or insight; challenge or correction. Areas of change may include salvation or spiritual growth; relationships to others or self; vocation or ministry; outlook or attitude.

DISCOVER

1. Distribute copies of MTM-3 and pencils to members. Have them pair off and work together. After reading the passage, they should list characteristics of each individual before and after encountering Christ. Tell them to consider the person's status, direction in life, spiritual condition, and so on. This exercise should not be hurried; tell members to look carefully at the impact of Jesus Christ on these lives, including their own. Partners should also share the answers they write to the two questions at the bottom of the page.
2. When you see that the pairs have finished, direct attention back to the lists on the chalkboard. Say: **What needed elements did Jesus bring to these persons? How would you describe the change that took place?** Invite a few to share answers about themselves.

RESPOND

1. Say: **Peter, the leper, the paralytic, Matthew, and I hope, each of you, have been changed in significant and permanent ways by encountering Jesus. No doubt, there are other changes He wants to make in you. Catch a vision of the new you as those changes occur, and let it**

motivate you to cooperate with Him. Spend the last part of the session praying with and for your partners and the changes yet to come for the both of you. Pray to be trusting and pliable as He works in you.

2. As the pairs pray, erase the chalkboard, and print: REJOICE! EVERY CHANGE THAT JESUS CAUSES IN US MAKES US MORE LIKE HIM.

3. Ask a group member to pray briefly to dismiss the group when pairs are done praying.

ASSIGNMENT

1. Have everyone read the board before leaving.

2. Ask group members to read chapter 5 of the text and Luke 6 for the next session.

SESSION 5

So What's New? Everything!

TEXT, CHAPTER 5

A QUICK LOOK

Session Topic   Jesus tells us what attitudes make for a life of blessing.

Session Goals   You will help group members:
1. Admit that sometimes what we've always heard isn't the truth *(Focus)*.
2. List ways to promote correct attitudes toward circumstances, others, ourselves, and God *(Discover)*.
3. Change attitudes and lifestyles in order to know blessings as the Lord intends *(Respond)*.

GETTING READY

What You'll Need
Bible
Be Compassionate
Paper
Pens or pencils
Chalkboard
Chalk
VS-1

Getting Ready to Teach
1. Read chapter 5 of *Be Compassionate* and highlight the author's main points. Read Luke 6.
2. The text mentions three new spiritual entities to replace that which was "worn out" in the Jewish religion: a new sabbath, a new nation, and a new blessing in the new spiritual kingdom. This session, however, will address the last of these points.
3. Before the session, reproduce VS-1 on the chalkboard.

THE LESSON

FOCUS

1. As the session opens, have a volunteer give two pieces of paper and a pencil to everyone.

2. Say: **Today we will have a pop quiz to test your knowledge of medical folklore. As I read these familiar statements, write true or false for each. Save one piece of paper for later.** (Give the answers at the end.)

- ☐ An apple is nature's toothbrush (F).
- ☐ Eating chocolate causes acne (F).
- ☐ You'll catch a cold if your feet get wet (F).
- ☐ It's unwise to drink liquids while exercising (F).
- ☐ Natural vitamins are healthier for you than synthetic ones (F).
- ☐ Aristocrats have blue blood (F).
- ☐ Getting a bad sunburn is a quick way to a tan (F).
- ☐ Freezing foods kills bacteria (F).
- ☐ A smile uses fewer muscles than a frown (T).
- ☐ It's unhealthy to drink water that comes from the bathroom sink (F).
- ☐ Eating green apples gives you a bellyache (F).
- ☐ You can prevent catching a cold by wearing a hat (F).
- ☐ Black coffee sobers you up (F).
- ☐ The more you cut your hair, the faster it grows (F).

3. If you wish to give the answers concisely, simply say that only the statement about a smile using fewer muscles is true—all other statements are false. Explain that many of these statements are very familiar. Many people have heard and supposed them true for years.

4. Invite comments and discussion—not on the statements you read—

VS-1
The group will form four smaller groups by deciding which of these attitudes they want most to improve in their lives.

To live a blessed life, have correct attitudes toward

Circumstances— faith in God in all circumstances. Luke 6:20-26	People—show love to them. Luke 6:27-38
Ourselves— honesty with ourselves. Luke 6:39-45	God—obedience, not lip service. Luke 6:46-49

21

but on the fact that things we have heard over and over are not always true.

DISCOVER

1. Make a transition explaining that the world has been telling us for years through these nuggets of folk wisdom how to stay healthy. At times, its advice has been off the mark because it wasn't based on fact—just the best guess men could come up with. Point out that the world has also dispensed a lot of misinformation over the years about how to live a blessed life. Ask: **What are some things you must have or do in order to be blessed in this life, according to the world?**

2. Tell group members that Jesus came to set the record straight about living a blessed life. Point to chalkboard. Explain that Jesus said to have correct attitudes toward:

☐ *Circumstances*—having faith in God for all circumstances;
☐ *People*—showing them love;
☐ *Ourselves*—being honest with ourselves;
☐ *God*—giving obedience, not lip-service.

Say: **Think about which of these attitudes is hardest for you to reach, or in which you'd most like to see improvement. You will be joining with others who choose the same attitude you do, in order to arrive at practical ways to promote the attitudes Christ wants for us.**

3. Indicate where in the room the four respective groups will meet. When members are settled, give these instructions: **Read your group's passage; then fashion six practical ways to promote a correct attitude toward circumstances, others, self, or God. Remember—unless an idea is something you can and actually will do in the coming week, it won't help you much; so choose these actions well. Write down the ways for yourselves so you have a copy.** Allow 15 minutes for this exercise.

4. Join the smallest group and take part yourself.

5. When groups have finished, ask for their six ways to promote correct attitudes that will result in blessed living.

RESPOND

Members should remain in their groups to pray together for success and motivation in carrying out their ideas during the week. Their goal will be to start promoting correct attitudes toward circumstances, others, self, and God—wherever they feel the weakest.

ASSIGNMENT

Have members read chapter 6 from the text and Luke 7 for next week.

SESSION 6

Compassion in Action

TEXT, CHAPTER 6

A QUICK LOOK

Session Topic   We learn to respond to people in need by following Christ's example.

Session Goals   You will help group members:
1. Become aware of different needs that people have *(Focus)*.
2. List guidelines or actions Jesus used in helping others *(Discover)*.
3. Practice using these guidelines and actions *(Respond)*.

GETTING READY

What   Bible
You'll Need   *Be Compassionate*
                    Copies of MTM-4
                    Pencils
                    Chalkboard, chalk

Getting Ready   1. Read chapter 6 of the text and Luke 7.
to Teach   2. Make copies of MTM-4 for group members.
                  3. Last week, the four small groups made lists of practical activities their members could do to promote correct attitudes toward circumstances, others, self, and God. You will start the session by asking if anyone tried the activities and has something to share with the group. This means that you personally will need to follow through with your list so that you can be the first to share. Since life application makes the lessons stick, urge members

23

(without nagging or inflicting guilt) to practice what they learn during the week.

THE LESSON

FOCUS

1. Greet members as they arrive. Start by asking who followed through on last week's list of activities and has something to share. You will go first.

2. Have a member distribute copies of MTM-4 and pencils. Tell group members that you want them to begin thinking about this session's title, "Compassion in Action." Have group members read the four situations on MTM-4 and answer the questions as honestly as they can. Tell members that they won't be asked to show their answers to anyone. Great detail is not necessary. Allow up to 15 minutes to complete the questions.

3. As group members work through the exercise on MTM-4, put these headings across the top of the chalkboard: CENTURION; WIDOW; JOHN THE BAPTIST; SINFUL WOMAN. Then make yourself available to help or encourage members.

DISCOVER

1. Say: **Let's leave our four case studies for a while and look at Jesus' encounters with some needy people in Luke 7.** As a group, read the following passages and look for guidelines and actions in Jesus' responses to the centurion, the widow, John the Baptist, and the sinful woman. Explain that you are looking for general guidelines which can be applied today as you minister to others in need. List replies on the chalkboard under the proper heading as members give them.

☐ Have a volunteer read Luke 7:1-10. Ask: **From the way Jesus dealt with the centurion's need, what guidelines or actions, however simple, can we find to use when someone asks for our help?** (For the centurion passage, guidelines or actions could be: Jesus listened to the request; saw a sincere attitude; responded positively to his show of faith; granted the request.)

☐ Ask another member to read 7:11-17. (Possible guidelines or actions: Jesus felt the pain of the widow with her; comforted her; did something to meet the need.)

☐ Have someone read 7:18-23. (List guidelines like: Jesus helped John review the facts of His ministry; brought Scripture to bear on the problem.)

☐ Ask someone else to read 7:36-50. (General guidelines could include: Jesus received and acknowledged her love; did not "preach" at her; re-

■ **Elizabeth, John the Baptist, Mary** **Their basic response:** _____
(Luke 1:39–56)

In Mary's song, the Magnificat, she magnified God because He had done what things for which parties?

■ **Zacharias** **His basic response:** _____
(Luke 1:57–80)

What do you suppose occupied Zacharias' thoughts during the time he was speechless prior to John's birth? Why do you think so?

MTM-2 Use with session 3 of *Be Compassionate.*
©1988 by SP Publications, Inc. Permission granted to purchaser to reproduce this visual for class purposes

(Luke 5:17-26)

Matthew
(Luke 5:27-39)

You

What further changes does Christ want to make in you?

What will you be like then?

The Favor

A friend asks you if you would drive his brother to the airport for a midnight flight. A sudden family matter prevented him from doing it as planned. Without presuming your answer, he shows you a map with the route from your house to where his brother is staying to the airport, plus the departure time and flight and gate numbers. How do you respond to his faith in asking you this favor?

The Darkness

A single woman in your apartment building is nearly blind. Without family or friends—now unable to live alone—she is filled with despair. How do you respond to her despair?

MTM-4 Use with session 6 of *Be Compassionate*.
©1988 by SP Publications, Inc. Permission granted to purchaser to reproduce this visual for class purposes.

A. Who is your neighbor? To whom are you a neighbor?

B. Have you made a practice of ignoring anyone? If so, why?

C. Why does being a neighbor always involve sacrifice?

■ III. Worshipers (Luke 10:38-42)

A. What does "Take time to be holy" mean to you?

B. Is busyness a problem in your life? If so, what can and will you do about it?

C. List your seven top priorities in life in order.

ENCOURAGEMENTS TO PRAY

1 Jesus tells us how. Read Luke 11:2–4 and skim the section titled "Pattern for Prayer" from chapter 10 of the text. Personalize the Lord's Prayer by writing it in your own words.

2 God rewards persistence. Read Luke 11:5–8 and 18:1–8. Describe how these passages make you feel about praying.

What do you think Jesus meant by being "rich toward God"?

WORRYING (Luke 12:22–34)
A tearing apart, a being held in suspense. Using the Scripture and the section about worrying in chapter 11 of the text, list what worry does and doesn't do. Write Luke 12:35 in your own words.

CARELESSNESS (Luke 12:35–49)
How ready are you for Jesus' return? Would He find you waiting and watching, working and warring at His second coming?

DON'T DELAY—
ACCEPT TODAY!

The Tower Tragedy (Luke 13:1-5)

What point did Jesus make here? What impact did it have when He personalized His remarks and warnings to those present?

The Fig Tree (Luke 13:6-9)

Read Matthew 3:7-10. What are the implications for believers who bear no fruit? In their case, what does "cutting down" mean?

MTM-8 Use with session 12 of *Be Compassionate.*
©1988 by SP Publications, Inc. Permission granted to purchaser to reproduce this visual for class purposes

The Narrow Door (Luke 13:22-30)

What reasons does Wiersbe suggest for the Jews waiting so long to join the kingdom of God? (See "A Theological Question about Salvation," chapter 12 of the text.)

Jesus' Sorrow for Jerusalem (Luke 13:34-35)

Hebrews 4:7, citing Psalm 95:7-8, reads, "Today, if you hear His voice, do not harden your hearts." Wiersbe says in his own words, "The longer sinners wait, the harder their hearts become." Why?

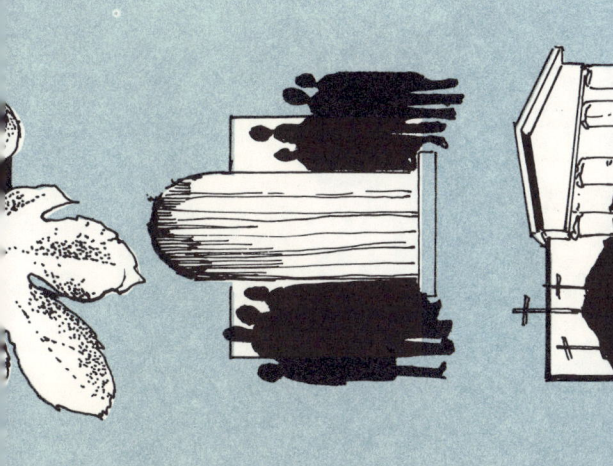

JESUS' FOUR WARNINGS

HYPOCRISY (Luke 12:1-12) Playacting, as actors speak in dialogue; hence, pretense.
Cause: fear of man (Matt. 23:27-28)
Cures: fear God alone (Luke 12:4-5); confess Christ (Luke 12:8-9); depend on the Holy Spirit (Luke 12:11-12). Why must these three cures work together against hypocrisy?

COVETOUSNESS (Luke 12:13-21) Unquenchable thirst for getting more and more.

3 God gives good gifts. Read Luke 11:11-13. Name some of the good gifts He has given you.

4 Jesus promises success. Read Luke 11:9-10. Wiersbe points out that the verb tenses mean "Keep on asking," "Keep on seeking," and "Keep on knocking." What have you given up too soon asking for, seeking, and knocking on doors for? What prayers should you start making again?

Be encouraged to pray faithfully. The answers may be closer than you think.

YOUR PRESENT THREEFOLD-MINISTRY EVALUATION

- I. **Ambassadors** (Luke 10:1-24)

   A. Have you been commissioned an ambassador? How do you know?

   B. Do you view yourself as a laborer? If so, in what way?

   C. What exactly do you have to offer the world?

The Degree

A college student attending your church confides to you that, halfway through his program, he wonders if he's pursuing the right degree. The course work is crushing, his interest wavering, and postgraduate job prospects in his field will be dim for years to come. How will you respond to his doubt?

The Return

A week ago your best friend seemed to drop out of sight. You don't know if you hurt her by something you said or did—you just miss her. Today she comes by, her old cheerful self, and brings you cookies she baked. She obviously wants to make up with you. The two of you have a fun day strolling around the mall like you used to. How do you respond to your friend's love?

MTM-3 Use with session 4 of *Be Compassionate.*
©1988 by SP Publications, Inc. Permission granted to purchaser to reproduce this visual for class purposes or

CASE: Jesus vs. Unbelieving Jews

Witnesses to the divine sonship of Jesus Christ
1. John the Baptist (Luke 3:4–6, 16–17)
2. Holy Spirit and God the Father (3:22)
3. Satan (4:3, 9)
4. Scripture (4:17–21)
5. Demons (4:33–34, 41)

How do these witnesses authenticate the divine sonship of Jesus?

Why is each a significant witness?

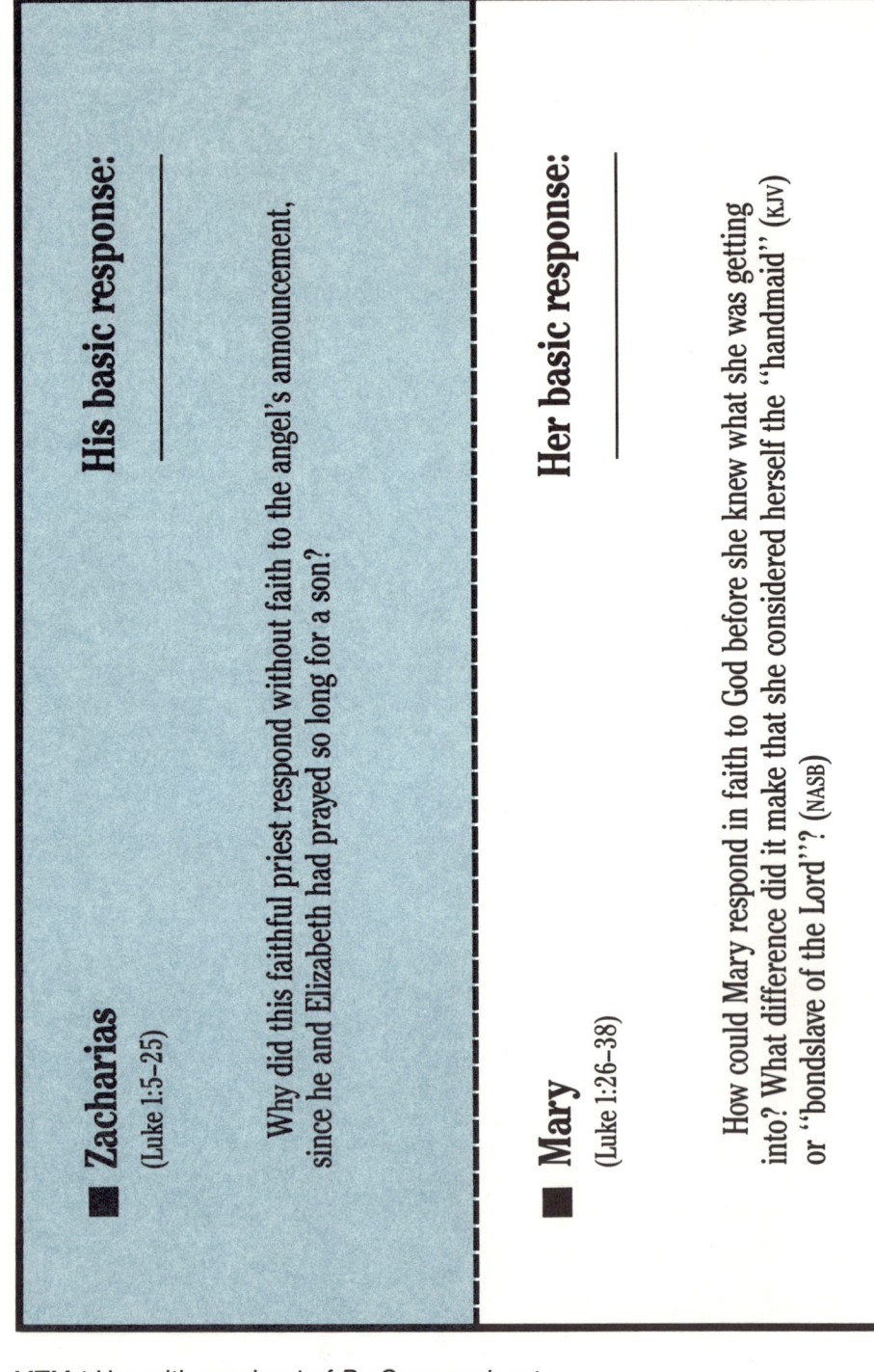

■ **Zacharias**
(Luke 1:5–25)

His basic response: _____

Why did this faithful priest respond without faith to the angel's announcement, since he and Elizabeth had prayed so long for a son?

■ **Mary**
(Luke 1:26–38)

Her basic response: _____

How could Mary respond in faith to God before she knew what she was getting into? What difference did it make that she considered herself the "handmaid" (KJV) or "bondslave of the Lord"? (NASB)

turned love to her.)

RESPOND

1. Say: **Let's go back to the four situations on the worksheet. In order to practice these actions, we will do some short, spontaneous role plays of these situations using what we drew out of Jesus' responses. Feel free to also include things you wrote on your sheets that would be helpful, such as, getting more information or praying with that person. But be especially mindful of using the items listed on the chalkboard.**

2. Call for two volunteers to role play "The Favor." When they have finished, ask the rest of the group which actions they noticed the players using. Thank your volunteers. Ask for others and handle the rest of the role plays in like fashion.

3. Urge members to keep these helping guidelines and actions in mind when they meet persons in need. Ask someone to close by praying that all will respond with "compassion in action" when needs arise.

ASSIGNMENT

Have group members read chapter 7 of the text and Luke 8 for next week.

SESSION 7

Lessons about Faith

TEXT, CHAPTER 7

A QUICK LOOK

Session Topic   The preparation of the soil of the heart is an important part of one's conversion.

Session Goals   You will help group members:
1. Admit the significance of how our hearts are prepared for the Gospel *(Focus)*.
2. List ways that unprepared soil can be made ready *(Discover)*.
3. Use their knowledge in practical ministry *(Respond)*.

GETTING READY

*What
You'll Need*
Bible
Be Compassionate
Chalkboard, chalk
Paper, pencils

*Getting Ready
to Teach*
1. Read chapter 7 of the text. Also read Luke 8 and Acts 10:1-2, 30-46.
2. In the Focus section, you will ask members to share how the Lord prepared their hearts to hear and accept the Gospel. As always, you will go first; so recall your initial contact with the Gospel, the condition of your heart, and the preparation God put it through that led to your conversion.
3. If your church keeps a guest register, find out if a committee follows up these guests.
4. In keeping with the theme of the soil of one's heart receiving the seed of the Word of God, dress like a

farmer or gardener (overalls, boots, feed-store cap, flannel shirt, and so on).
5. Write these three headings across the top of the chalkboard: PHARISEES/TEACHERS—Luke 5:21; 6:11, 7:30; SHALLOW DISCIPLES—John 7:52-66; RICH YOUNG RULER—Luke 18:18-24.
6. Make two copies of the skit in the Focus section of session 8. At the end of this session find two men to prepare the skit and give them the copies.
7. Congratulations! You are halfway through the study of *Be Compassionate* (Luke 1–12). Continue to give your best effort to preparing each session and to coming spiritually ready yourself. Pray. Encourage members in their attendance, participation, and application of what they learn. And be encouraged yourself. May God work through you to plant His Word in members' lives.

THE LESSON

FOCUS

1. Explain to the group that you didn't dress in farmer's clothes for no reason at all. Say: **I'd like to share with you about the condition of the soil of my heart when the seed of the Gospel first fell on it.** Share briefly the state of your heart, how you heard the Gospel, and your reaction. If you didn't accept Jesus at first, tell how God prepared your heart for that.
2. Ask for four volunteers (one at a time) to share the same things about themselves for a couple minutes each. Thank each for sharing.

DISCOVER

1. Say: **Our sharing of experiences shows that, despite the different stages of hardness or rockiness or thorniness in the soil of our hearts, God prepared them to receive the seed of His Word in faith and to produce. We'll look at some hearts today that were ready, and some that weren't.**
2. Have someone read Acts 10:1-2, 30-46 aloud. Use the following questions to guide your discussion of this passage:
☐ **What about Cornelius indicates he was ready for the Word of God?** (He was devoted, led a God-fearing family, prayed regularly, gave to the poor, was eager to listen to Peter.)
☐ **What happened the minute the seed of the Word of God hit the soil**

of their hearts? (Cornelius, his family, and friends received it, were converted, and the Holy Spirit came upon them.)
☐ How does Cornelius' story relate to Romans 10:14-15, 17?

3. Have the members divide into three discovery groups. Give each group a piece of paper and a pencil and have them choose a secretary. Assign each group one of the parties on the chalkboard. Groups should read their passages and identify the condition of their parties' hearts. Then, through discussion, appropriate Scripture, and applying the personal sharing that members did in the Focus section, groups should find ways to build up or minister to those who have hard, stony, or thorny hearts.

Allow 15 minutes or longer if groups need it; follow with reports from each group. During the reports, jot down key phrases on the chalkboard under respective headings.

RESPOND

1. If groups mention that inviting someone to church is a way to prepare his heart for the Gospel, use that point for your springboard. Say: **Many churches ask newcomers and visitors to sign the guest register. The result is a list of individuals about whose needs and spiritual condition the church may know little or nothing.** If your church has a committee that follows up on newcomers and guests, challenge your group members to take part in this ministry, even for a short time. If no guest register or follow-up committee exists, suggest that members volunteer to the pastor to help begin them.

2. Point out that among those who sign guest lists are persons who heard God's Word but have no depth yet. Unless they are drawn into the church and their faith strengthened, they might give up during trials. There might also be individuals whose faith is being choked by worries, riches, and pleasure. They too need fellowship of other Christians in order to make trust in God a habit and spiritual matters a priority. Of course, sometimes people who don't believe attend church. They might never believe until someone gives them attention and helps them plow up the hardened soil of their hearts.

3. Close in prayer, asking God to motivate all to want to build up the faith of weak or wavering believers; and to want to cultivate the soil of hearts that don't yet know Christ.

ASSIGNMENT

1. Have group members read chapter 8 of the text and Luke 9.
2. Give copies of the skit for session 8 to two male volunteers to prepare.

SESSION 8

A Many-sided Ministry

TEXT, CHAPTER 8

A QUICK LOOK

Session Topic   Busy Christians put Christ and His kingdom first.

Session Goals
1. Determine the importance of taking time out for Christ's kingdom *(Focus)*.
2. Evaluate one's busyness and priorities in life *(Discover)*.
3. Commit daily schedules to the Lord for the sake of His kingdom *(Respond)*.

GETTING READY

What
You'll Need

Bible
Be Compassionate
Chalkboard, chalk
Paper, pencils

Getting Ready
to Teach

1. Read chapter 8 of the text and Luke 9.
2. Evaluate your own priorities, busyness, and willingness to serve God's kingdom. Complete the exercise in *Discover #3* regarding your schedule and priorities.
3. Before the session starts, write these activities on the chalkboard: EATING; SLEEPING/NAPPING; READING NEWSPAPERS/MAGAZINES; WORK/SCHOOL; DEVOTIONS; SHOPPING; HOUSEHOLD CHORES/PAPERWORK; WORKING IN THE YARD; COMMUTING/TRAVELING;
4. Call your two volunteers about the skit for the Focus section. Offer help if they need it. Suggest that they come early to practice. If possible, bring a

45

hedge trimmer as a prop.

THE LESSON

FOCUS

1. Introduce the players in the skit and have them begin.

[*This scene takes place in Henry's backyard near his neighbor's fence. Henry is busy trimming his imaginary hedge, humming as he works; Fred, the neighbor, walks up to the other side of the hedge, looks over, and startles Henry.*]

Fred: Hi, Henry!
Henry: Oh, hi, Fred. Boy, I didn't see you there. Nearly had me a heart attack. [*Chuckles*]
Fred: Sorry, didn't mean to scare you. Just thought I'd come over and say hello. Nice day, huh?
Henry: Sure is. Perfect day for some yard work. I've got a hundred things to do before my daughter's graduation party next Sunday.
Fred: Yeah, well, I uh—[*Hesitates*] I don't want to keep you but I was wondering . . . Well, never mind. Hope you get a lot done. See you later, Henry. [*Turns and slowly walks away.*]
Henry: [*Pauses to think, looks over the hedge at Fred.*] Say, Fred. [*Walks around the hedge.*] I'm not too busy for a neighbor. Did you have something on your mind you wanted to talk about? Is it your wife's cancer?
Fred: Yeah, that's it, all right. It has been one very rough week for her. I feel like I need to talk to somebody. The cancer has made her very weak. The doctors say she may only have a few weeks left. I feel like both of us are at the end of our rope. Yes, I know she'll go to be with the Lord but—what am I going to do without her? [*Places hand over eyes, lowers head.*]
Henry: [*Puts his hand on Fred's shoulder and speaks gently.*] Come on over and sit with us for a while. [*They walk off toward Henry's house together.*]

2. Initiate a discussion with the following questions:
☐ **What alternatives did Fred have if Henry hadn't taken time to meet his need that day?**
☐ **What was Henry thinking when he decided to reach out to Fred?**
☐ **What results, do you suppose, came out of this situation for Fred? For Henry?**
Make these points if group members do not:
☐ Fred may have felt all alone in that painful experience if Henry hadn't responded.
☐ Henry may have asked himself at that moment what Christ would

have wanted him to do.

=== DISCOVER ===

1. Instruct the members to silently read Luke 9:10-17, 37-45. Ask them for a simple statement describing what the passages have in common besides miracles. (In both cases, Jesus went the extra mile to meet a pressing human need.) Discuss the passage using the following questions as a guide:

☐ Was it Jesus' fault that so many people followed Him uninvited into a remote place without bringing food along? Was it Jesus' responsibility to feed them?

☐ What can we tell about Jesus' attitude toward the people, especially from verse 11?

☐ In the other passage, was it just another interruption in Jesus' schedule that a man in the crowd stopped Him to beg for help for his son? In what way was it more than just another interruption?

☐ People were always wanting something from Jesus; how did He respond to this need? How did He turn what seemed like interruptions and intrusions into kingdom opportunities?

2. Read aloud Luke 9:57-62. Ask: **What conflict was Jesus talking about in this passage?** Start a discussion of the passage regarding daily duties and busyness, and service in the kingdom of God. Ask: **What does God see as our priorities in life?** Ask members to silently answer this question for themselves: **Are you feeling the conflict between taking the time to serve the Lord and meeting the daily demands of your schedule?**

3. Hand out paper and pencils. Instruct members to make a thorough list of all the events, activities, tasks, and so on, that are part of their average week. They should include and add to the list you began on the chalkboard. Allow at least 10 minutes for them to write their lists. When you see that they have finished, read the following questions and instructions:

☐ In all honesty, which tasks or activities in your weekly schedule would you interrupt to answer someone's request for help? To take a lengthy phone call from a person in need? To put yourself out in order to minister to someone who was hurting?

☐ Put a checkmark (√) by those things. (*Pause a minute.*)

☐ Now put an X by those things you'd really prefer not to interrupt for those reasons. (*Pause.*)

☐ Ask yourself: In my list of activities, have I programmed any time especially for ministry? Or have I blocked out some time to allow flexibility in my schedule for unexpected ministry opportunities? (*Pause to allow for reflection.*)

☐ Is your #1 priority Christ's kingdom over any and all weekly tasks or

happenings? (*Pause.*)
☐ Would your attitude toward ministry be better if you just weren't so busy? (*Pause.*)
☐ Is busyness really the problem? What is?

4. Members have been silently thinking over these questions thus far; now reread them one at a time beginning with "In all honesty." Call for members to share their thoughts, insights, examples, or problems they faced in answering. Do not be judgmental, but accept all contributions and encourage introspection.

5. When the discussion draws to a close, reread Luke 9:57-62 aloud.

RESPOND

1. Instruct members to pair up to pray with and for each other, dedicating their daily schedules to the Lord for the sake of His kingdom.

2. Close in prayer, thanking God that He always has time for us, and praying that members would decide they always have time for His kingdom.

ASSIGNMENT

Have members read chapter 9 of the text and Luke 10 for next week.

SESSION 9

What in the World Does a Christian Do?

TEXT, CHAPTER 9

A QUICK LOOK

Session Topic   Every Christian has a threefold ministry while on earth.

Session Goals   You will help group members:
1. Design a meaningful logo for the threefold ministry of a Christian *(Focus)*.
2. Evaluate their present participation in the threefold ministry *(Discover)*.
3. Set goals for growth and make necessary changes toward the threefold ministry *(Respond)*.

GETTING READY

What
You'll Need

Bible
Be Compassionate
VS-2
Copies of MTM-5
Chalkboard, chalk
Tables, chairs
Crayons
Paper, pencils, tape

Getting Ready
to Teach

1. Read chapter 9 of the text and Luke 10.
2. Work through the lesson and be prepared with your own answers and ideas for MTM-5.
3. Take time to pray about your ministry in the world, using your discoveries from MTM-5 as a guide.
4. Make two copies of the skit in the Focus section of session 10. You will give them to two volunteers at the end of this session so they can prepare for the

following week.
5. Make copies of MTM-5 for members.
6. Set up tables and chairs. Place a good supply of crayons (or colored markers) on each table.
7. Copy VS-2 on the chalkboard.

THE LESSON

=== FOCUS ===

1. When members arrive, direct them to be seated at the tables. Distribute blank pieces of paper and pencils.

2. Ask someone to read aloud Wiersbe's introduction to chapter 9 of *Be Compassionate* (first three paragraphs).

3. Say: **Welcome, Delegates, to the First Annual Threefold Christian Ministry Convention.** Refer to the chalkboard. Continue: **I'm glad you could attend. We have much to accomplish today, so let's get started.** Instruct delegates to carefully reread Luke 10, focusing on the threefold ministry of the believer. Refer to the three points on the chalkboard: Ambassadors, Neighbors, Worshipers. Tell delegates that they may take notes on those ministries as they read.

4. When delegates are done reading, say: **Our first task will be to design and draw a logo for the threefold ministry. Your logo should reflect the ministries graphically or symbolically. You will have 5–10 minutes to work, but give it some thought before you start drawing so that your logos are meaningful. From your creations, we will choose one design that best captures the threefold ministry.**

5. In 5–10 minutes, ask for volunteers to briefly show and explain their logos. When all who wish to show their logos have done so, have the

---

Welcome to the First Annual Threefold
Christian Ministry Convention!

Ambassadors
Neighbors
Worshipers

VS-2

delegates vote for the logo that best represents the threefold ministry. Tape that logo to the board beside the words Ambassadors, Neighbors, and Worshipers.

DISCOVER

1. Next, distribute copies of MTM-5.

2. Say: **Now, Delegates, we will move to the second phase of the convention. We will evaluate our own present ministry to the world in order to be better equipped for the future. Take 15 minutes to individually work through the questionnaire. We'll talk about it later.**

3. When the delegates have finished, initiate a discussion using the questionnaire as a guide. It is important that you have worked through it yourself in advance. Bring in appropriate Scripture or refer to the text if you wish.

RESPOND

1. Say: **I want to thank you delegates for your hard work and contributions to the convention. We are now entering the final phase. Please look over your evaluation questionnaire and circle items that trigger ideas for better ministry, or remind you of changes you should make, or reveal problems you should deal with. After that, make a list of those ideas, changes, or problems on the back of the questionnaire to use during our prayertime.**

2. When you see the delegates finishing their lists, direct them to pair up, share their ideas, changes, and problems, and pray over these matters. Also, challenge group members to turn their ideas into goals, and the needed changes into reality.

3. As you dismiss the group, say: **Thank you, Delegates, for taking part in the First Annual Threefold Christian Ministry Convention. May the Lord help you accomplish your goals, make necessary changes in your lives, and find solutions to your problems.**

ASSIGNMENT

1. Tell members to read chapter 10 of the text and Luke 11 for next week.

2. Ask two members—a man and a woman—to prepare a short skit for next week. Give each a copy of the skit.

SESSION 10

Learning Life's Lessons

TEXT, CHAPTER 10

A QUICK LOOK

Session Topic   Jesus leaves His followers powerful encouragements to pray.

Session Goals   You will help group members:
1. Admit that meaningful encouragements help them do what is difficult *(Focus)*.
2. Uncover the encouragements Jesus gives them to be faithful to pray *(Discover)*.
3. Determine to be faithful to pray for matters they have given up on *(Respond)*.

GETTING READY

What You'll Need
Bible
Be Compassionate
Newspaper, dish towel, dish
Copies of MTM-6, pencils

Getting Ready to Teach
1. Read chapter 10 of the text and Luke 11.
2. Again this week, the chapter from Luke has several topics presented through Jesus' teaching—prayer, Satan, opportunity, and hypocrisy. Rather than attempting to link them into a cohesive lesson and deal with each adequately, this session will concentrate on Jesus' teaching about prayer (11:1-13).
3. Make copies of MTM-6 for the group.
4. Remind your skit volunteers with a call. They may practice by coming 15 minutes early. Exact memorization is not necessary if they act convincingly and deliver the message of the skit.

5. Before the session begins, put a couple chairs in the front of the room for the Husband.
6. Bring simple props, such as, a newspaper, a dish towel, and a dish.
7. You will close the session by singing "God Is So Good." If you will not lead the song, find someone to do it for you.
8. Make two copies of the skit directions in the Focus section of session 11. Find two persons to prepare the skit—a man and a woman—and give each a copy at the end of this session.

THE LESSON

FOCUS

1. Say: **If you've ever had a hard time motivating yourself to do something you know you should do, perhaps all you needed was the right encouragement.** Introduce your players and let them begin.

[*The skit opens with the Husband seated, reading a newspaper, feet up on a chair. The Wife enters with a dish towel and dish in her hands.*]

Wife:	Sweetheart, didn't you say you were going to start cycling again? The weather's getting nice.
Husband:	[*Lowers paper and sighs.*] Yes, I did. I just need to get going, that's all.
Wife:	Once you get into a routine, you'll feel a lot better about exercising. Besides, you only have a few pounds to lose.
Husband:	Yes, but it's so hard to get motivated to ride by myself. I wish you liked riding too.
Wife:	Say, why don't you and Don ride together? Rosemary said he was going to ride to the river and back three nights a week.
Husband:	Now that sounds interesting, but I'll still have to get the serial number from the bike and register it at the police department.
Wife:	I took care of that for you today.
Husband:	Thanks, Honey. Now all I have to do is clean up the bike and put air in the tires.
Wife:	I did that today too. You're all set. Gonna call Don?
Husband:	Hmm . . . I'm thinking . . .
Wife:	I'll tell you what. If you start riding with Don three nights a week, I'll sew you a pair of riding shorts and a top to match.
Husband:	It's a deal! [*They shake hands, laughing.*]

2. Thank your players and have them be seated. Ask: **Exercise is still exercise, but how did this man's thinking about the cycling program**

change? Explain that the wife did two things to encourage her husband and promised to do another. Ask: **Do incentives which involve delivery tomorrow motivate us today?** Ask group members to explain their answers. (Remember—in the discussion sections, you want members to interact with one another, not just direct answers to you. Try to get group members listening and talking to each other.)

DISCOVER

1. After members have aired their ideas, point out that the man in the skit had a familiar problem: he knew he should be exercising but, because he had been away from it for a while, he found it hard to start again. Ask: **Which Christian discipline does this sound like?**

2. When someone says "Prayer," continue: **That's right—prayer. Of course, Jesus knew this about His followers, and so He left them valuable incentives to pray in Luke 11. To get better acquainted with these incentives, you will work through this sheet individually. Later, we'll share as a group.**

3. Distribute copies of MTM-6 and pencils. Be available to encourage and answer questions as group members work through the MTM. When members have finished, direct them to form groups of three to share their responses among themselves.

RESPOND

1. When you see that the sharing time is ending, say: **The last question on the sheet asked you what things you had given up asking for, seeking, or knocking on doors for. Sometimes we should give up because God is saying no. Other times we should either give up or change our motives because we are asking with wrong motives. Other times, though, we are asking according to God's will with the right motives, and He fully intends to answer yes; but like the man who went to his neighbor for bread, we must persist. Pray with and for one another in your small groups about those requests you gave up on, but for which you believe God will still have answers. When you leave today, be encouraged to keep praying until He answers.**

2. When you see the groups finishing, begin to sing softly "God Is So Good," especially the verse beginning "He answers prayer."

ASSIGNMENT

Have group members read chapter 11 of the text and Luke 12.

SESSION 11

Believer, Beware!

TEXT, CHAPTER 11

A QUICK LOOK

Session Topic   Jesus warns His followers against sins that will cripple their faith.

Session Goals   You will help group members:
1. Recognize how easily sin can creep into Christians' lives *(Focus)*.
2. Study the four warnings Jesus gave His followers *(Discover)*.
3. Evaluate their own lives and heed Jesus' warnings *(Respond)*.

GETTING READY

What You'll Need
Bible
Be Compassionate
Copies of MTM-7, pencils
Masks for Focus section
VS -3

Getting Ready to Teach
1. Read chapter 11 of the text and Luke 12.
2. Make copies of MTM-7.
3. You will need to make masks for your players in the skit in the Focus section. These masks will be reminiscent of those used in ancient Greek theater. From a piece of poster board cut a life-size shape of a head and color its features. You need one smiling face and one frowning face for both the man and the woman in the skit—four in all. Cut out the mouth and make small holes to see through. Finally, attach a handle to the mask so that it can be

held in front of the face. (See VS-3.)
(NOTE: Give the players freedom to come up with several conversations. The skit should last a couple minutes. Remember—the Hs are believers but they have let sin creep into their lives.)
4. Call your volunteers during the week to see how their preparation is coming. Offer help if they need it. Have them come 15 minutes early to practice with the masks. Place two chairs in the front for them.
5. Unrecognized sin or unrenounced sin is a serious matter in any believer's life. Examine your own heart in the course of lesson preparation so that you can lead your group members in their self-examination.

THE LESSON

FOCUS

1. Say: **Born-again Christians, though grace through faith has saved them, still sin. When sin gets a toehold in their lives, it can become a part of their lifestyle, and, therefore, hard to detect—at least for the believers themselves.**

I'd like you to meet Mr. and Mrs. H, Christians who have been members of Central Bible Church for 10 years. Today they are attending a church social. Let's join them.

> This is the scenario. Mr. and Mrs. H are seated at a church social. Now and then imaginary church members walk by and chat with them. At these

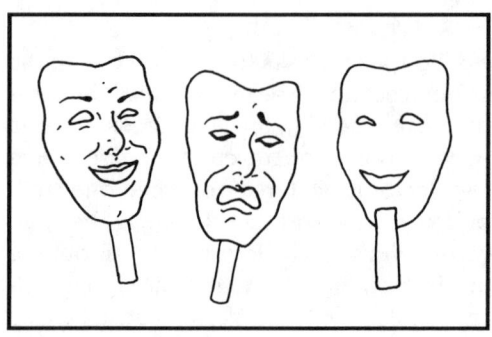

VS-3
These front and back views of the masks will help you know how to make them.

times, the Hs hold up the smiling faces and speak warmly and sincerely. When the imaginary persons leave, the Hs put up the frowning faces and speak their true thoughts. For example: "Hello, Edna; that dress really fits you" is followed by "Where did she get that thing—from a tentmaker?" Or "Bill, we've been praying for you and the planning committee" followed by "Man, that's one guy I can't stand—he's such a phony."

2. After the skit, thank your players. Then ask the following questions:
☐ What was Mr. and Mrs. H's most evident problem?
☐ Do you suppose they are aware of it? Why or why not?
☐ If this sin goes unchecked, what could be the effect on their witness and personal faith?
☐ Of course, no one is obligated to answer this next question, but ask yourself honestly: Did I see or hear myself in the skit?

DISCOVER

1. Point out that in Luke 12, Jesus warns His followers to beware of allowing sins to creep into their lives; in particular, hypocrisy, covetousness, worrying, and carelessness. To help group members understand these warnings better, have them work through MTM-7 in teams.

2. Divide the group into three smaller groups and distribute copies of MTM-7 and pencils. Remind group members to look up all the references. Then say: **When you reach the last question on the page, answer it only to yourselves.**

3. When you see that the groups have worked through the handout and have paused for individuals to reflect on the last question (about 15 minutes), continue. "Walk through" the worksheet as a group, helping the group digest its own answers and comments and to resolve its own questions. Try to wrap up discussion in 15 minutes.

RESPOND

1. Say: **The best response anyone can make to Jesus' warnings is to heed them.** Therefore, take a few minutes now to look into your lives to detect hypocrisy, covetousness, worrying, or carelessness, or any sin for that matter.

2. In a few minutes, direct members to pair up to pray with and for each other regarding their areas of weakness. Tell them you'll close in prayer in a few minutes. Do so, asking God to forgive, encourage, and strengthen members to avoid sin. Thank Him for the ministry of His Word.

ASSIGNMENT

Have members read chapter 12 of the text and Luke 13 for next week.

SESSION 12

Questions and Answers

TEXT, CHAPTER 12

A QUICK LOOK

Session Topic Individuals are responsible for answering the invitation of God while there is time.

Session Goals You will help group members:
1. Recognize the danger of waiting too long to accept an invitation *(Focus)*.
2. Catch the urgency of responding to God's invitation *(Discover)*.
3. Accept any outstanding invitations from the Lord *(Respond)*.

GETTING READY

What You'll Need
Bible
Be Compassionate
Copies of MTM-8
Pens or pencils
A record album of a musical
A piece of firewood

Getting Ready to Teach
1. Read chapter 12 of the text and highlight the author's main points. Read Luke 13.
2. Make copies of MTM-8.
3. Bring an attractive record album of a musical and a piece of firewood to display as props during the Focus section. They will help group members concentrate attention on the case studies you read.
4. As you come to the close of this study, pray for your group members. Ask God to help them apply what they have learned through this study.

58

THE LESSON

===== FOCUS =====

1. Place the record album in front where all can see it. Read the following case study:
>   Central College was casting in the fall for its spring musical. Three talented senior voice majors were the obvious choices for the leads, and they knew it. The director asked them early to play the leads and had reminded them a few times about his deadline for casting. However, the seniors, who hung around together, put the director off, failed to return his calls, and joked about playing hard-to-get. Finally they went to the director's office, only to learn that he had given the leads to other vocalists. He said, "I hadn't heard from any of you by the casting deadline, so I chose three other students who've been calling me daily about those parts. Sorry." The seniors were furious.

2. Ask: **What were the seniors wrongly assuming? How did the assumption affect their response?**

3. Take the record album down and display the piece of firewood. Read the following case study:
>   Old Mr. Tucker was eager to clear a piece of his property of trees. So he told his neighbor, Mr. Jackson, that he could keep the firewood if he cut the trees down. That sounded like a good deal to Jackson, only he wasn't in any hurry to do the job. Day after day for months he drove past Tucker's property; the standing timbers looked like money in the bank to him. Then one day, Jackson saw a crew of men felling, cutting, and hauling the trees. He shook his head and slammed the steering wheel with his fist. "I'll be burning my own money this winter instead of Tucker's wood," he thought.

4. Ask: **If Jackson knew Tucker wanted the land cleared soon, why did he delay? What do you think about Tucker calling someone else for the job?**

5. Place the record album next to the piece of firewood. Discuss the case studies using these questions as a guide:
   ☐ **What are the similarities in these case studies?**
   ☐ **What did you detect in the attitudes of the senior vocal majors and Jackson?**
   ☐ **Have you ever made a similar mistake? What did it cost you?** (If you have made such a mistake yourself, be willing to share first. Allow a few members to share briefly, but only if they wish to.)

===== DISCOVER =====

1. Say: **As we have seen and experienced, if we delay accepting invitations and going through open doors, often the invitations go to other people, and the doors close to us. Whatever loss we suffer, though, it is**

59

never as great as the loss suffered by those who ignore the invitation to enter the kingdom of God; that is, to enter by placing trust in Jesus as Savior. In Luke 13, Jesus shook up His listeners by teaching that God's patience wouldn't last forever; neither would they have infinite time to respond. Today we will pool our thoughts and observations by working through the handout together.

2. Distribute copies of MTM-8 and pencils. Ask for readers when you come to Scripture passages. Remember: as members offer answers, comments, or personal experiences, try to get them listening and talking to each other.

3. When the group has worked its way through the handout, ask: **What kind of risks do individuals take by ignoring God's invitation to enter His kingdom? What risks do fruitless believers take?**

=== RESPOND ===

1. Ask group members to take a few moments to reflect as you read through the following suggestions for meditation:

☐ In Luke 13, Jesus was addressing the Jews as a nation and individually when He urged them to accept the invitation to the kingdom. There is application today to any person who has not entered God's kingdom by trusting Jesus as Saviour; also to Christians whose lives still haven't borne the fruit God is looking for. (*Pause.*)

☐ If you haven't accepted God's invitation to His kingdom and want to talk to me afterward about it, I'll be available." (NOTE: Use your judgment in saying this, since you may already know the lives and spiritual commitment of the group members.)

☐ If you feel that you should be producing more fruit in your life, read Galatians 5:22-23 right now. See the fruit God desires, and examine the fruit you've been producing. (*Pause a minute.*)

☐ Decide to accept any outstanding invitations from God to undertake, to receive, or to be something. Determine to go through any door He's holding open for you. (*Pause.*)

2. Instruct members to find a partner to pray with and for concerning any outstanding invitations and the quality and quantity of fruit in their lives. After a few minutes, close in prayer, asking for God to encourage group members to respond now to all invitations He gives them.

=== ASSIGNMENT ===

1. Tell members that next week will be a review session of the entire book *Be Compassionate*. They should come with favorite topics, unan-

swered questions, and newly discovered insights in mind.

2. Ask for some volunteers to bring simple refreshments, like coffee or juice, rolls or doughnuts.

SESSION 13

Review

TEXT, CHAPTER 1–12

A QUICK LOOK

Session Topic   If we live what Christ teaches in Luke 1–13, we will be compassionate.

Session Goals   You will help group members:
Review *Be Compassionate*, Luke 1–13, and what they learned in the course of the study.

GETTING READY

What You'll Need
Bible
Be Compassionate
Refreshments

Getting Ready to Teach
1. Skim through *Be Compassionate*, Luke 1–13, and your personal notes. Come with something to share.
2. Coordinate refreshments with members who volunteered to help.

THE LESSON

This lesson will not be as structured as past sessions, but it will be an excellent chance to pull teachings together, deal with loose ends and questions, and hear how the study has benefited the members.

Start with refreshments and keep the atmosphere informal. After 10 minutes or so, invite the members to bring their refreshments with them and be seated.

Explain that the review session will have roughly three sections:
☐ *Favorite topics or lessons*—reviewing will help the lessons stick;

☐ *Unanswered questions*—perhaps some members have questions from past sessions that haven't been answered yet;

☐ *New insights*—let members share what they have learned and how they have become more compassionate.

Follow the flow of the conversation and enjoy the fellowship.

Notes